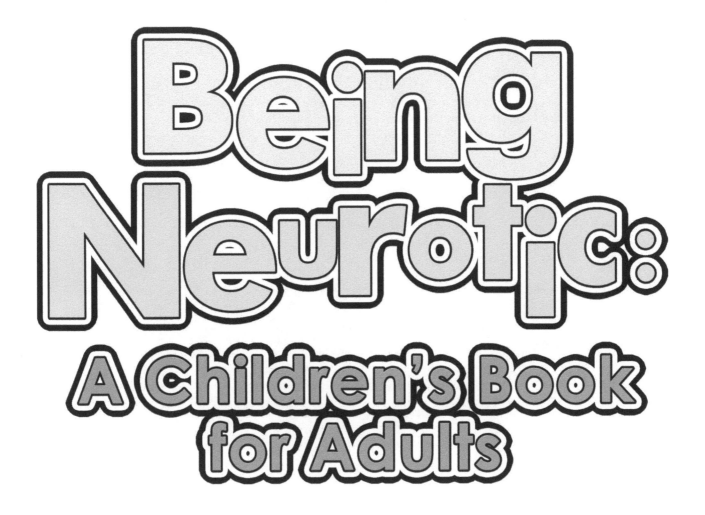

Dr. Terry Bordan

Archway Publishing books may be ordered through booksellers or by contacting:

Archway Publishing
1663 Liberty Drive
Bloomington, IN 47403
www.archwaypublishing.com
844-669-3957

Because of the dynamic nature of the Internet, any web addresses or links contained in this book may have changed since publication and may no longer be valid. The views expressed in this work are solely those of the author and do not necessarily reflect the views of the publisher, and the publisher hereby disclaims any responsibility for them.

Any people depicted in stock imagery provided by Getty Images are models, and such images are being used for illustrative purposes only.
Certain stock imagery © Getty Images.

ISBN: 978-1-6657-2508-8 (sc)
ISBN: 978-1-6657-2506-4 (hc)
ISBN: 978-1-6657-2507-1 (e)

Print information available on the last page.

Archway Publishing rev. date: 09/01/2022

Always for my Ted of blessed memory
who loved me neurotic warts and all

A Children's Book for Adults

People tell us that we act like children so we deserve a pretty book with a glossy cover and really cute illustrations that we can use as our bedtime story. It also can be used as a unique coffee table book – guaranteed to start a lively conversation!

Contents

intro (might be slightly boring, feel free to skip if so inclined)

If you bought this book or are only perusing it while checking out the titles in the bookstore or more probably on-line, welcome to the club. It's a wonderful club; wear your membership with pride. We are the "garden variety neurotic". When describing conditions, it is often asked what is the typical age of "onset" (in other words, when did being neurotic begin?). Well with us, it is at any age; although truth be told our "condition" does seem to worsen with age. The possibility of leaving the club is very poor … but truth again be told, we are charmers who delight and mystify others while we may make it rather uncomfortable for ourselves from time-to-time.

So, let's begin by defining "neurotic". You know that term was used quite a bit in the past; nowadays, one rarely hears it. I remember when it was sort of a badge of honor … He's so neurotic; she is so neurotic …. But usually followed with: they are so much fun. And, we are! Let's remember that as we read through the rest of this book. Back to definitions: The dictionary defines it as "an emotionally unstable individual (no wonder we have so many hang-ups – let's throw that one out right now)". As an adjective, it is "of, relating to, constituting, or affected with neurosis." And we really love this one: it can be used as an adverb, like "neurotically". So, we guess you can say that we all behave "neurotically". Well, lucky us! See, that is the first step in living a happier life; it is understanding that we can and must shed any negativity that is connected with the word neurotic. It's a lot of malarkey or bunk anyway. Good. Now let's continue.

So the following chapters will discuss issues, feelings, fears, etc. that may be commonplace for those of us who wear the mantel of the neurotic one. If there is one thing that I hope that you take away from your reading it is that what you experience is shared by so many. You are not alone out there and need not feel that you are crazy. As a matter of fact, if you think that you are nuts, YOU ARE NOT! There, it is stated and will be our mantra. There is a book that is the bible for all mental health practitioners: it is the *Diagnostic and Statistical Manual of Mental Disorders* (DSM-5). Guess what? If you look in the index in the back of said tome, nowhere, I repeat, nowhere is the word neurotic mentioned. So there! Back to our mantra: if you think that you are nuts, you are not!

Now, as the author (sometimes I will refer to myself in the third person – perhaps another of our traits – maybe. Being somewhat indecisive may be another.) As a retired college professor, I cannot help but include a little history here with regard to the use of the word "neurotic". In the past, anxiety disorders were classified as neurotic behavior and textbooks had a field day going over all the symptoms that this supposed patient would exhibit. Well, the *DSM-5,* as stated previously, does not call them neuroses any longer! See, we are well on our way to being legitimate. I don't really have a copy of the latest DSM (too expensive to purchase for this one time mention – come to think of it, frugality may be somewhat descriptive of our condition) but I cannot imagine that the word "neurotic" has enjoyed any kind of comeback.

Now, let's go even further back in time: "Neurosis" as a term was first used in 1769 by an Englishman, William Cullen. Those darn Brits! It basically had to do with abnormalities of the nervous system. Then along came Freud who defied this explanation and stated that neurotic behavior had nothing to do with the nervous system per se but was caused by intrapsychic (million dollar term for inside your head) conflict. All of a sudden it became a psychological problem. Freud went on to say that there was an internal fight between the id, that primitive part of the brain that just wants and wants and wants and wants anything and everything, here and now, this instant, and the ego and superego that are there to warn and act as the bad cop so to speak so that the poor little id can't have its way. A by-product of all of this was anxiety. According to Sigmund, sometimes people were aware of this inner turmoil but for the most part they were not. It didn't matter: either way it was supposedly the root cause of all of this neurotic activity.

Okay, so we have pretty much dropped all that, but we are still left with some people bantering about "neuroticism" as some kind of personality trait associated with negative behaviors. Give me a break! So, I will break free from the chains and indignities that history has attributed to neurotic tendencies remembering that the term "neurosis" is considered obsolete. We retrieve this beautiful term from some graveyard where psychological terms no longer in existence reside and use it as a wonderful descriptor. We will learn to celebrate our behaviors and find them to be charming, a tad eccentric, but all the while making us worthy for anyone to get to know us better. If there is one thing that can be said of us, it is that we certainly are not boring. We are charming, adorable neurotics (CAN) ... So let's add one more thing to our mantra: we are not nuts and we certainly CAN do whatever it is we like (well, okay within reason; there are some activities that can get you arrested or shunned – we don't want that.).

If you are not sure if you qualify for our wonderful club, here is a little quiz for you to take to determine how neurotic you might be:

You know you are neurotic when:

1. You apologize to the chairs that you bump into. (Silly question; it doesn't even count in scoring – someone highly neurotic begged me to include it.)
2. You stress so much when filling out standardized forms that you have to take a Xanax to compose yourself.
3. You don't walk the dog in the cold for fear that she will develop pneumonia and then give it to you.
4. You spend hours reading golf magazines and selecting the perfect putter only to freeze up on the course and hit your ball into a water hazard.
5. You plan a wonderful vacation to Australia then freak out because your luggage may exceed the size or weight limits.
6. You switch between two pairs of glasses because you can't manage the challenge of bifocals.
7. You are the only one wearing slip-on slippers in the airport security line.
8. You have created five different Facebook accounts and then stress out when trying to figure out who is who among your multiple screen identities.
9. When traveling you get stopped by airport security for having too many bottles of pills in your bag.
10. You cannot listen to anyone's symptoms without immediately identifying with them.
11. If you listed your fears and worries, you would run out of paper.
12. Your fear of dying is much greater than your fear of death … and the later is pretty big.
13. Having to use a public restroom requires a series of moves that might qualify you as a gymnast for the Olympics.
14. If you grew up hearing about superstitions (usually from mother), it is impossible not to follow any ritual necessary to ward off evil spirits.
15. If you see a picture on the wall that is slightly crooked, you feel compelled to fix it. By the way, 94% of the population has some unwanted, intrusive thoughts. So a little obsessive compulsive disorder (OCD) is no big deal!
16. If a loved one is in the bathroom for more than three minutes, you yell out "Are you all right?"
17. You not only talk to plants but you argue with them. If it's a debate, you lose.
18. You are like Rodney Dangerfield … you get no respect.
19. You read the fairytale "The Princess and the Pea" and it seems autobiographical to you. Is there anything that doesn't bother us?

If you answered "yes" to at least five questions, you are slightly neurotic and will enjoy the book. (Remember question #1 doesn't count for scoring.) If you answered "yes" to eight to twelve questions, you are definitely neurotic and will relate well to this book. If you answered "no" to all questions, you definitely need the book because you are a neurotic who is in denial! How do I know that you are neurotic? I know you are neurotic because you bought the book in the first place.

Anxiety: "What, Me Worry?" Alfred E. Neuman (Mad Magazine)

Al (I feel that we are on a first name basis) emerged in an ad for painless dentistry in the late nineteenth century. So many good people have been trying to calm us down for centuries without much success. Worry. What an interesting word. "To feel uneasy or concerned about something, be troubled" can be found in the dictionary under "worry". They tell us that worry is part of the "human condition". Well, that certainly makes us feel better. Misery does love company. Our worries tend to bleed into our lives and cause us to feel not so good about ourselves or what may be going on. Worries cross over to anxiety too often in our lives. Way too often.

They (who are "they" anyway) also tell us that worry can be helpful. It is a call to action when something needs to be addressed or fixed. Ha! For many of us, it is a call to do nothing … our energies are exhausted by worry or anxiety. According to Dr. Luana Marques, "Anxiety is your body's natural threat response system. When your brain believes you are in danger, it sends out a series of signals to your body, resulting in the fight-or-flight response." So anxiety is a reaction to something that we perceive to be dangerous or frightening. I love it when we get all preachy and professorial. Well, we are cured now that we know it is natural and helpful. Yeah, right! Our bodies have telegraphed that message to us too often that many of us go around shell shocked. How many of us jump when the phone rings? Shell shocked is another old-fashioned term. Soldiers, themselves, coined the phrase. It was used when a soldier was no longer able to do his duties or function and no reason could be determined to be the cause. I guess Al could have said "What, me shell shocked". No, that would never have made it into popular lexicon. Now where were we?

I am so tired of being worried or anxious. As Madeline Kahn sang in "Blazing Saddles", I am tired of being tired. But, tell the truth: it does help to know you are not alone. So when someone says to you "Will you please stop your constant worrying about something?" or would you "Quit being so nervous. You are making me nervous with your being so nervous!" or "You are just plain nuts!" You now can respond with something like, "It is my body's natural reaction to what is going on in my head as I am perceiving something that I am worried about as a threat." That ought to do it. Yeah, right!! We are just an example of a garden variety neurotic.

Best ways to manage anxiety and stress

Take breaks from watching the news
Take care of yourself
Do breathing exercises
Meditation
Exercise
Sleep for 7 hrs at night
No drugs or alcohol
Talk to others about what is causing you stress

Please don't get me wrong. Sometimes if the worry or anxious feeling is very troubling, it can be helpful to seek medical attention. Good ole' talk therapy with or without medication may be just what is needed. So if you are: very restless; easily fatigued; having difficulty concentrating or your mind just goes blank; very irritable (who isn't from time to time, but this is truly different); have muscle tension; and sleep disturbance, please seek some help if you have at least three of those six symptoms. You would be amazed how much help is out there.

So when our Alfred E. Neuman asked "What, me worry?" our answer is "Yes". We worry, but we are okay with it. It has not disturbed our day to-day functioning. We are still good (well, good is a relative term). Let this book serve as a social support gift. You now know that you are most certainly not alone. There's even someone such as myself who is willing to write about it and tell the world all her eccentricities. Love euphemisms, don't you? Eccentricities, what a beautiful word.

So let's get rid of all our "what ifs". That's right, we "what if" all the time. And don't forget that we catastrophize with our "what ifs". So throw the "what ifs" out; do not speak it; do not think it. Easier said than done, right? We have to challenge our thoughts and our ways of thinking. But that is for another book.

Let's end this chapter on a breathing technique that many of us have found to be helpful:
1. You exhale completely through the mouth making a whooshing sound.
2. Close mouth (get your foot out first) and inhale quietly through the nose to a mental count of 4.
3. Hold breath for a count of 7.
4. Exhale completely through the mouth making another whoosh sound to a count of 8.

That is considered to be one breath. You can do a 4 breath cycle twice a day BUT never more than 4!! We don't want light headedness or passing out that we have deliberately done to ourselves. We do enough to ourselves with our thoughts and behaviors – no need to add additional misery.

It's Not Easy Being a Hypochondriac — We Are Exhausted

First, let's state the obvious: whenever you hear about side effects of medication, be it on TV, radio, or simply listening to a person speak about what might happen if you take a drug or what to look for if you have a certain condition (we dare not call it disease – much too frightening), we must immediately put our two index fingers (that means both hands) in our ears and say aloud, "La, la, la, la, la, la, la, la, la ..." until those "symptoms" are no longer mentioned. Never ever listen; you know that if not that day, very soon (usually within 48-72 hours), you will be experiencing what was discussed. The only way to attempt to avoid this is simply not to hear – not give your brain a chance to seed the thought that, "YES that is what I am going through."

Side effects: Have you ever listened during a commercial for a drug product what may occur if taking said medication. What don't they list: Headaches (pounding, blinding of course); bleeding from every orifice possible; nervousness (that's all we need to add to our general anxieties and worries); dizziness; trouble sleeping; dry mouth; nausea; tummy upset; diarrhea; blood pressure (too high, too low, too unstable); fast pounding heart beat (been there, done that); swollen glands; confusion; need to seek immediate medical assistance; rash, trouble breathing; and death (of course). I could go on and on but why bother. We get the drift; we got it. Yes, WE GOT IT. Put us on a new medication, and we promise you, we will get side effects ... especially those that are rare and dangerous. All we need do is read the warning packet that comes with the new drug. Why, oh why, do we have to read that pamphlet? Haven't we learned not to fill our heads with suggestive details about what may happen? Simply for us to read it guarantees that it WILL happen.

It goes without saying (but we must say it) NEVER resort to looking things up on the internet. Our eyes are immediately drawn to the worst case scenario. If it states that this symptom could be the cause of something horrendous or lethal, it doesn't matter that that sentence is followed up with stating that only .00002 of the population who experiences whatever, might have this. We got this. You know when we hear the statement, "Don't worry friend, you got this", said to us for encouragement, we turn it into "We've got this". And this is bad, very bad. So a rule: do not go to the internet EVER. The internet can turn an average headache into something that requires an emergency consultation with a neurologist – no, make that a neurosurgeon.

We need each other. The only person who will listen to us complaining about the latest in what we think we have are other hypochondriacs. Our other members of any other support or social network that we have, have long ago abandoned listening to our complaints. They are tired of our going to them asking if they think what we have is ... anything. They have long ago exhausted checking out a part of our body so that we can display our latest skin condition, pimple, or rash. We have forfeited our dignity many years ago. At the beginning of our becoming one of the "worried well", we would never expose a private part of our body. Now we would go up to a stranger if we needed reassurance that whatever is on our body is not indicative of what will be a terminal condition. We have no dignity; we have no shame. Remember the old days when the physician would come into the room with our folder so thick with all the times that we have complained about anything remotely medical. Now everything is on computer, so we are spared one less indignity. We don't care that it takes many minutes for our doctor to peruse what is on the computer in the room.

It is so fatiguing to always be imagining that we are dying. We don't waste our worry time on anything that is treatable, curable, and of very little consequence. It is so difficult as we go from disease and illness to disease and illness with very little time in between when we can feel "safe". I am tired just writing about it. Can you imagine the energy we use with worry after worry about imaginary illness? When it is all over (usually requiring a dismissal from a credible health care professional), we breathe a sigh of relief. We are fortunate if we can get a couple of days of not worrying about something going on in our bodies. Usually we don't have that long. We certainly don't have as much as a week before we are ruminating about something else medical. We are so good at that: ruminating, obsessing. We get a hold of a worry, and we don't just think about it for a moment. We obsess and think and re-think about it ad nauseam. It goes without saying how COVID has made that so much more pronounced. Why can't we just stop it?! Just stop it! I refer you to something funny and possibly quite helpful, Bob Newhart on YouTube – just google on YouTube "Bob Newhart Stop It". Stop reading and do that right now!

Seriously (are we ever) if your preoccupation with your medical fears about having a serious (using that word twice-must mean business) disease gets to be too much, please seek medical attention. Once you do and you are still preoccupied and need more reassurance, please continue to seek assistance. If these fears impair your social or occupational life, again seek some help. Finally what you may be experiencing is a type of generalized anxiety disorder, obsessive-compulsive disorder, panic disorder, separation anxiety disorder, or depressive disorder. We need a professional to help us figure this out. But if you are simply a member of the worried well, highly neurotic club, you now know you are not alone. That should be helpful. Yes?

Bathroom Practices: The Good, the Bad, the Ugly

Come on you didn't think that I wouldn't have a chapter on bathroom habits in a book for the neurotic. We know that we all have them ... maybe ours are a bit more than most .... this isn't necessarily a bad thing.

The first rule is that you never, ever, never use patterned toilet paper. It is too easy to forget that there is a pink rose on the sheet. You are in a hurry; you forget; and then, almost pass out when you casually glance down and see "red". I would avoid beets for the same reason. Don't roll up your eyes ... you know that this could be you. So only white, soft paper will do for the seriously neurotic. As an aside, a problem seems to exist with two-ply toilet paper. It may not dissolve properly in the water and thus cause an overflow. So my suggestion is simple: if you are going to use two-ply, wait until the toilet stops flushing before walking away. Obviously, I am referring to your own private bathroom or that of a friend's. If you are in public, the aforementioned does not apply. One last caveat: if you use one-ply, you must double up and use twice as much .... No yukky hands for us.

Let's now talk about public toilets .... We must; sorry! Second rule: always have sanitizing wipes, spray, or bottle on your person. I know that I am preaching to the choir here, but it never hurts to emphasize sanitation of any sort. I think it best to go step-by-step in planning to use a public facility. We need to plan this like Sherman taking Atlanta. We are at war with germs and battle we must. Let's forget that Sherman ultimately burned down Atlanta. Our first skirmish would be with the door leading to the bathroom. Is it a push/pull or does it have a doorknob? The later is much more of a challenge for us, so let's tackle the former first. Well maybe we should do the later first. No, I think it best to do the former ... I think. Sound familiar? Some of us can decide on something really big almost immediately, but the small stuff really gets to us.

How many can relate to being in a restaurant and taking ages to decide what entrée to order? We try to be the last to order so that we can hear what everybody else wants. Everybody knows better than we. Might I digress (which is often what we do)? I was about to go on a rant about all others picking a better entrée, and this is supposed to be a chapter on bathroom habits or etiquette.

Okay. We are at the push/pull door. We push with either an elbow or our back. Both need to be clothed in order to protect the skin from touching the germ infested door. A doorknob door requires a bit more gymnastics. Always good to have a disposable tissue that you use to work the door. Our movement is similar to what we see on crime shows where the detective takes out his latex (always check for allergic reactions to common products!) glove and ever so carefully picks up the knife, gun, other murder weapon, or suspicious clue and deposits same in a plastic baggie. We will be depositing ours in a nearby wastepaper basket. Better yet, keeping it in our hand so that we may use it to open the stall door. Gents, you are on your own here if no stalls! I was thinking of doing some reconnaissance so that I could be more specific about what the guys might have to do, but I was deterred at the last moment for fear of getting arrested. I thought that might hurt my chances of getting this handbook of sorts published. Now back to business: We are now safely inside the stall and with our hands delicately pull down any undergarments that need to be removed in order to do … well you know what we have to do. Number one is easy; number two requires some upper and lower dexterity on our part. More about that in a minute.

Okay we are now ready to squat in the most awkward squat ever asked of humankind. In no way can we allow any part of our body to touch a public toilet. Hey, we may do the same when at a friend's, family member's, and/or stranger's restroom. Isn't that a curious word for toilet? There is no rest for the weary here. We need strength in our knees, thighs, and legs to accomplish what is a Herculean feat: coming nowhere near the seat of the toilet. You know other countries call a "toilet" a "toilet". As a matter of fact, if you asked someone in another country, "Where is the restroom?" they may look at you quite puzzled. But I digress (common trait among the neurotic). Do you know that the Queen of England has a lady- in- waiting (and wait she must) who carries a toilet seat around for the Queen's personal use? Oops, I am digressing again. Can't seem to help myself!

Now, where were we? Yes, we are in the midst of describing a 90 degree squat performed with shaky legs, thighs, and knees. We must hope that this job does not take too long. We shake and get shakier by the second. We are incentivized to hold that now 45 degree angle a little bit longer. To fail is not an option. Could you imagine falling down and actually touching the seat? I cringe as I write about this.

Now, if you feel that you cannot depend upon your lower extremity to do its job, you may have to resort to doing what you would have to do if you were doing a number two: line the toilet seat. This requires extreme dexterity. You must somehow hold the paper between fingers and let it "float" onto the seat. Sometimes this "float" is not successful and it "floats" into the water. You must be ready to try again immediately. I know there are bathrooms (another silly name for toilets).… We aren't going to a public toilet to take a bath! So silly. Where was I now? Yes, explaining about seat covers that may or may not be available in individual stalls. Are you supposed to take out the middle piece that seems to be cut already or does that piece fall out by itself if something a tad heavy falls on it? However if you are using said paper to line the seat instead of your doing it by hand for a number one, nothing heavy will be going on it. You understand. Now the same delicate maneuvering that you would use if you were taking the toilet paper off the roll to line the seat yourself, must be employed. When doing it oneself, we are now talking about minimally triple layering; thus, you need to make sure your stall has sufficient paper on the roll.

By the way, getting it off the roll is no easy feat. You tug, you pull, you touch gently, you touch brutally; it can be ever so hard to get that roll started. Don't roll your eyes. You know I speak the truth. You never, ever, ever, ever use the first few squares of the toilet paper that is on the roll. It has possibly been touched by a stranger whose hygiene is an unknown. The first few (few being defined by the individual's need for mental comfort) sheets go right into the toilet bowl. Now we are ready to gather just enough toilet paper to accomplish our aims (pun intended). Some people are "sprayers" … You know who you are! Others are straight shooters (pun again intended). We now finish our business and with shaky legs, stand upright and do our best to finish the job so that we leave the stall with clothing both cleaned and appropriately returned to its best position.

I remember seeing a woman at an airport who looked like she came off the cover of Vogue magazine. Image ruined by her having toilet paper stuck to her shoe as she walked. She finally noticed or some good Samaritan told her that she had a new appendage and then she began the "put one foot almost directly in back of the other in order to step on paper that is then removed by stepping on the paper and taking a one step stride to leave toilet paper on floor and not shoe" cha-cha-cha. There I go, another digression. Hope that you have a smile on your face as you so identify with the situation. See, already you are happier that you are not alone in what is in your head or in your somewhat eccentric actions. Back to where we were. Where were we? On to the actual flush.

We have left the stall and are approaching the sink. No, no. We must back up before we exit the claustrophobic cage of the stall, we must flush the toilet. We again ask a lot of ourselves. We need to flush the toilet without using our hands. We need to take one leg and steady ourselves as we lift said leg to hit the "flusher thing" (is there a real word for it?). Success, toilet flushes and if we are lucky, all contents that we have contributed to the bowl flush along with the flush. If doing a number two, we will have to lift our leg and do a circular motion with our leg as we barely touch with the sole of our shoe the toilet paper or ready made toilet seat cover thing that was offered up in order for us to line the seat. You know the kind mentioned previously with the middle almost cut out but not quite. All needs to go in toilet before it is successfully flushed. I know I used "flush" twice in a sentence (or did I?), but I needed to be direct in all of the aforementioned instructions or descriptions.

Now another problem that we often encounter is that of the automatic flush of the toilet when done. Sometimes the toilet flushes way before we have ended our session. With terribly shaky legs, we hold our angled position so that none of that tainted water touches any part of our sensitive skin and/or clothing. Now another option is that we are done, and it does not flush at all. How do we leave the stall with our dignity when the next person is headed right our way to use that very same stall? The answer to that question could not be simpler … We don't!

We have lost our dignity on many more occasions with people whom we know. That woman/man is a stranger. We will never see them again. Holding head high and resolute in our gait, we exit and begin the six feet sojourn to the sink. What can happen in a mere six feet? Almost forgot to mention another sort of "mishap". So let's go back to our being in the stall. I know we are jumping from subject to subject and not having any semblance of a linear tale but that is another thing we do all the time.

What if our aim has not been too good and the seat is wet. Do we clean it? That would require again taking quite a lot of the toilet paper and delicately, as we hold our breath and nose, wiping down the seat. Some of us do that; some of us do not. If you are in the later group, you must be prepared as you exit the stall, to look at the next occupant and say, with enough disgust but not too much, "You might want to use another stall. This one is filthy."

Okay now we are finally at the sink. I am exhausted just writing about our bathroom sojourn. Remember the old sinks: one faucet for hot; one faucet for cold. These faucets used to meet somewhere in the middle and become one faucet that combines both hot and cold. That's easy. You put your hands under the faucet and wash away. If too hot or too cold, you adjust the particular faucet to achieve the correct temperature. Of course, very often you have adjusted the wrong one and jump back to prevent being scalded. Strange how it was always the hot one that needed to be adjusted. Nowadays you have the automatic sink. Supposedly, all one need do is put one's hand by something that recognizes that a hand is there and the water turns on. Have you noticed that for us, our particular sink doesn't turn on? We see and hear our neighbors' sinks functioning well. Never ours! We wait for them to leave and change sinks to use the one that we definitely saw that works. Many times we then succeed at washing our hands; many times we leave mystified that we couldn't make any of the sinks operational. Don't worry - we have our sanitizing lotion with us so that we can leave this public restroom with clean hands ... as long as we don't touch the exit door!

One last gymnastic move is required of us. We push the exit door with our clothed elbow, and voila, we are out. But sometimes you have to touch a lever or knob, here is where we channel an Olympic gymnast as we put our left leg outstretched making a sort of inverted "V" with our bodies so that the door remains open, and we can shoot any last piece of paper that we may have used at the end of this protocol right into the wastebasket that, for some reason, is too far away to definitely make the basket. Nonetheless, we never pick up the paper that has fallen just shy of the basket mark. We quickly exit, breathing a sigh of relief, and go on whatever adventure awaits us for the rest of the day.

Notice that this chapter was very lengthy. I couldn't help it.

Golf: Don't

Let's talk about a sport and pretend we are athletic – I know we are not as we are too afraid of getting hurt

There are many things that one can do in life that bring pleasure, peace, and a feeling of personal success. Golf is not one of them for the seriously neurotic. It really is a strange sport anyway. There is a small white (although there are those who select a color that easily identifies this object as theirs) ball you stand and swing away at in the hope of hitting this small ball into a hole somewhere far away that you can't see when you are swinging away.

The first shot is called the drive, and the author believes that that is a correct name for the motion because what it accomplishes is that it drives you quite crazy. It seems so easy, but if you take up the sport late in life (we believe that past the age of three is too late), you will find yourself looking, feeling, and acting foolish and ultimately experiencing humiliation as you often miss the darn ball completely. We neurotics do not need to deliberately add anything that increases our level of anxiety. We can do that quite automatically and without premeditation. Golf is a premeditated crime against neurotics perpetrated by the neurotic himself/herself and exacerbated by others who are not neurotic and who play the game as if born to do so. So basically, steer clear.

If you doubt this, let's go over some of the simple rules of the game, and it will become apparent that this is something to avoid at all costs (and come to think of it, the game is quite costly). But remember, it will cost you more than money. What is the price of dignity going for these days? These rules were taken from the mini edition of *Golf for Dummies* by Gary McCord. If you doubt what I espouse in this chapter, you may go to the more complete *Golf for Dummies*. Why can't there be dummy books for people who are too dumb for dummy books? But I guess that is a question for a sequel. Yes, imagine the hubris that I am already envisioning a sequel to this book before completing many chapters. We think big in the neurotic world and why not? We can't get into more trouble than we already have. Thanks Gary McCord for helping our clan to fully understand our need to boycott this sport. He even begins by calling golf a maddening and hard game. Do we need anything else to drive us madder than our natural condition takes us? Point one made already.

Let's begin: the object of the game is to get this small white ball into a hole far away with as few swings as possible. You do this for either 9 or 18 holes or something in between if you are a "quitter" (nothing wrong with that in our book). Whoever has the lowest score wins. Now that part we kind of like because many of us usually accomplish a low score on games anyway. If you go no further than page five of Gary's book, you read that it is essential that you stay calm and relaxed and think of nothing else while you stand there in front of friends or strangers trying so hard to not make a complete or even partial fool of yourself. So let's examine the aforementioned point by point.

Stay calm. Have we neurotics ever been able to do that ... *ever*? If staying calm is something that you can relate to, give back this book immediately; it is not for you. We neurotics approach a state that may be close to calm usually with the help of a pharmaceutical. Stay relaxed. Please re-read the preceding sentences that cover what I think of that tip. Now we come to the piece de resistance -- keep your mind on nothing other than correct stance and contact with this inanimate object. Have we ever been able to truly concentrate and not have multiple, sometimes racing (not in the psychiatric sense – remember we are simply neurotic) thoughts? If we really try not to have the multitude of thoughts that are usually upsetting, distracting, and sometimes outright crazy, we then have a tune that goes through our minds and that's one brain radio that we can't shut off. So relax and concentrate is not for the feint of heart or the neurotic.

Now if we have chosen the correct club (if you are bound and determined to take up this sport even after the warnings of this chapter), I advise you to only have a few clubs to use anyway. Surely you can have more in your bag to look good, but if you only have a few to choose from it makes the decision of which club to use so much easier. Don't these golf enthusiasts realize that for us to make a decision about what entrée to order in a restaurant causes us to feel anxious? I know I mentioned this before but we do have a tendency to repeat ourselves. Do they really expect us to stand there and calculate how far we are from the hole, taking into consideration wind conditions, the terrain, how high and wet the grass is, and the built in hazards of any course? We still don't understand why they need to include bunkers, water, dents, debris, and any other element to make the game harder. It is hard enough if everything were flat and perfect. Mark Twain was right: "Golf is a good walk interrupted".

That brings us to another point: you can either ride in a golf cart or walk. Are they kidding about walking? We are exhausted before we have taken our first swing. Fretting, worrying, and fearing take a toll on our energies before we have found ourselves on the first hole of the course. And don't forget that hiding the fact that we are fretting, worrying, and fearful makes the toll even higher. We are so tired before we reach the golf course. So weary. The non-neurotic cannot understand or commiserate in the least. The neurotic golfer becomes friends with the golf cart. In fact, if the golfer is playing with like-minded neurotic players, she or he might be allowed to play pretend golf and simply ride the golf cart and not play. This will work as long as the golf cart remains on the golf course and is not taken onto the highway.

This brings us to another point: only play with the like-minded neurotic. It won't cure all the aforementioned nonsense but it may cut it down to the point where we do not have to leave the golf course and go immediately to an asylum (do not pass go and do not collect $200 – come to think of it, we are safer playing Monopoly).

Now we can have some fun on the course. If someone swings and cannot see where the ball has landed (for us, it is clear: the ball is still on the tee because we have swung and missed), this player is allowed to go and look for the ball. It is a sport to see men (women know better) searching for an indeterminate amount of time for a ball that typically costs less than a dollar. And believe us, search they do!

Oops, we have left out "teeing up". This is where you put something akin to a little stick in the ground, put your ball on it, and swing away. This is only permitted on your first shot per hole and is called the drive. We neurotics who are extremely anal (most of us possess this distracting personality quirk—isn't quirk a nice euphemism; we neurotics are particularly fond of that word – it makes some of our actions, thoughts, and feelings sound much less like a medical disaster and akin to something that can be quite charming, but we digress, another trait characteristic of our clan ... forgive the lengthy, confusing and worst of all possible run-on sentence) may take longer than most deciding just how high or low to make the tee, checking its height with our ball and making sure that our ball takes up only half of this height. The other players are lucky that we don't bring rulers, protractors, and flexible measuring tools to do so. Anal is as anal does. We amend the famous quote from the movie, *Forest Gump*.

Let's discuss scoring. For most of us, it is quite easy. If there is a maximum number of shots permitted per hole, we can fill in our scorecard immediately. Just write that number down for all the holes. It takes the guesswork out of scoring and having to contemplate how many shots you took per hole. Some people look so wistful when they do this. You can imagine their thoughts: "Well, let's see; I took two shots to get to the sand trap, and one to get out of it and onto the green, and three shots on the green – that makes six. Yes, I need to put a six on the score card." We neurotics however, are cool; our scorecard is already filled out with the maximum number. We need not stand around with our minds and eyes pointed to the heavens adding up our shots. We particularly like when the maximum number allowed is lower with some games. It takes us out of our misery much quicker per hole.

Oh another point: there are different pars for different holes: you can have par 3, par 4, or par 5. This number has been determined by how many shots an accomplished golfer would take to sink that small ball into that small hole on a particular hole. It is always assumed that this good golfer would only have to take two shots when on the green. That is called putting. You may remember that word from what is meant to be funny and for us often times serious: when we say that something is "driving" us nuts, someone may remark, "you don't have to drive, all you need do is putt". (Digression, I know, and none of us can help it.) Back to pars; it is totally irrelevant for us ... maximum number of shots is just the maximum number of shots. Although again the par 3's do take us out of our misery faster, and we get to walk less – yes, you have to walk quite a bit even if you have a motorized cart. It is so mentally and physically draining no matter how long or what the heck the par number is (Yes, I curse ... actually quite a lot, but I am trying to get this published. Can't afford to offend anyone).

Now another term that is familiar to us is "scramble". We usually use it when referring to the condition of our brains. In golf, it is a form of play: everyone takes his or her turn and then all move their balls to where the best, and usually the longest, shot has landed. It supposedly takes the pressure off of having to have each shot be glorious. Well maybe it takes the pressure off the non-neurotic, but for us there is no such thing as "taking the pressure off".

The USGA (United States Golf Association) has decided in its ultimate wisdom to employ a handicap system. Yep, you read right ... a handicap system. Like we really need someone to point out to us that our golf is sub-par (love that play on words). How does one arrive at the handicap score? You simply take the average of the best ten of your previous 20 scores. That's easy for us: we have the same score for each game – the maximum. Now the lower the handicap score, the better the player. For once we have earned a higher score than others in a game .... So what if it is not a good thing.

In golf, you may not speak or make a move when someone else is about to take a swing. I guess the inventor of the game never knew any agitated, impatient, or restless people. Can you imagine having to stand perfectly still and not be able to express the thoughts that are ever present in our heads? Who has that kind of patience? As if that isn't enough, you have to get a grip. We have been trying to get a grip our whole lives. Now they tell us it's mandatory. Fagetaboutit!

The Junior Neurotic: The Legacy Continues

Whole books are dedicated to individuals but this author (I know third person dialogue again) must acknowledge one specific person for this final short piece. The author has a nephew, Darrell, who serves as the inspiration and more importantly has displayed all the signs that are mentioned below. The neurotic legacy continues without interruption, dilution, or diminution. The heritage thrives!

You know when your toddlers have inherited your tendencies when the following happen:
    Asks to go to dentist
    Tells us that they need to go to the doctor to get medicine
    Asks for their temperature to be taken *rectally*
    Tells us that they need to use the thermometer to get the *poopies* out of the *tush*
    Alerts people to drive carefully because it is slippery outside
    Does not like to be dirty and actually asks for napkins when eating
    When given a box of chocolates, declines them for fear of choking
    States that they want to go brush their teeth in order to prevent cavities
    Won't walk in snow
    Asks for meds to help with cough
    Starts listing their fears and becomes hoarse from talking so much and so long

As people who are willing to declare proudly their membership in the club for the neurotic, Sonny and Cher would say "The beat goes on". We know it does because we often take our pulse to see if it is rapid!

"That's all Folks"
Porky Pig

I would like to request that you submit your favorite/weird/highly neurotic experience(s). After all neurotic can be a noun, adjective, and even an adverb. Please give permission to use your submission(s) with your name in the next book on being neurotic or feel free to state that you wish to remain anonymous. I hope to include these in a sequel. Yes, sometimes those of us who are neurotic think a little bit on the positive side ... sometimes ... but we are always humble. Here I am imagining another book and I haven't finished writing this one!

Please submit to:

neuroticbook@gmail.com

I am so excited to start reading your adventures. Thank you for reading mine.

CPSIA information can be obtained
at www.ICGtesting.com
Printed in the USA
LVHW072107160922
728596LV00002B/45